THIS IS ME: NEHEMIAH JAMES

WRITTEN BY BLANCA HINES
ILLUSTRATED BY JESÚS GALLARDO

Copyright © 2020 This Is Me: Nehemiah James
All rights reserved.

ISBN: 978-1-952779-12-1
Library of Congress Control Number: 2020921609

DEDICATION:

For Nehemiah James and Naomi Jordin. My two loves, you have made Mommy and Daddy the happiest parents in the world.

ACKNOWLEDGEMENTS:

To my husband, thank you for helping me raise these two beautifully mixed children and for your support during my new journey of being an author.

And Thank you to *Abuelitos* and G-parents, for respecting and embracing each other's cultures so our children could feel your unconditional love.

Hi Guys! I'm Nehemiah James. I have a mami, a daddy, and a little *hermanita*. *Mami* is the Spanish word for *mommy* and *hermanita* means little sister.

I was born in America and have TWO ethnicities. This means that I am made up of two races and cultures aside from being American. My *mami* is Mexican-American and my daddy is African-American.

My skin is light brown, like peanut butter. I love to eat peanut butter on my sandwich. Yum! My *mami* says I'm the perfect color mix of my daddy and her. I have really dark, curly hair like my daddy. Daddy takes his hair off with a razor, so he is bald most of the time. What kind of hair do you have?

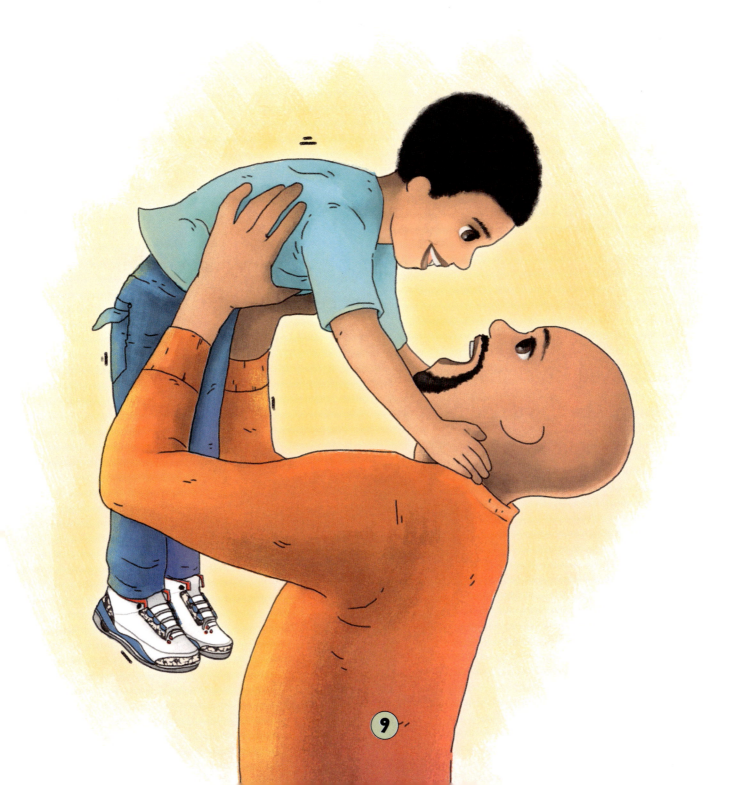

My *mami* and daddy are always taking care of my sister and me. *Mami* and Daddy also help lots of other people, too. I remember one time my daddy gave some food to a man who didn't have a home. Daddy prayed for the man so that God could help him find a home very soon. *Mami* and Daddy are my heroes! Heroes do great things for other people!

This is my friend Dy the dinosaur. I love dinosaurs, RAWR! He's my hero, too. Dy helps me understand Spanish sometimes, like when my *mami* asks me, "*¿Tienes hambre?*" He tells me that my mami wants to know if I'm hungry. I usually am hungry for yummy fruit! *¡Rica Fruta!* Dy says that means delicious fruit.

My *mami* is teaching me to speak Spanish, which is the language she speaks. My *abuelitos* speak Spanish, too. Dy helps me very much when I go visit my *abuelitos*. *Abuelitos* means grandparents.

Mami told me that one time, my *abuelita* helped a women who was very sick and made her feel all better. I always love hearing stories of heroes who do great things to make people feel good.

My *abuelito* was born in Mexico. He came here to America with his *mami* and *papi*. *Papi* is the Spanish word for *daddy*. My *abuelito* went to school here in America, but he had to quit college so he could work. He helped his *papi* buy food to help feed his brothers and sisters. My *abuelito* had to make a tough choice whether to quit going to school or not. In the end, he was able to help his family.

Wow! I can't imagine leaving my school to work all day! Can you? My *abuelitos* are my heroes! Heroes do great things to help their families!

I love that I am learning to speak two languages. Spanish is what my *mami* and *abuelitos* speak and English which is what my daddy and g-parents speak. My *mami* says it's important and very helpful to speak more than one language. This way, I can help anyone who only knows one language. How many languages do you speak? Maybe I can learn a lot more languages so that I can help the whole world.

My daddy's parents, who I call g-parents, lived during a very tough time in America. My daddy explained to me that when both my g-parents were my age, they had to help their families get through the separation between the different races that existed in their community. My g-dad played a big role in helping to keep his brothers and sisters happy during this time since he was one of the older brothers.

Daddy told me my g-parents grew up during the civil rights movement. He says he has lots of hero stories to share about them with my *hermanita* and I. My g-parents are my heroes! Heroes do great things to change the world!

Some of my favorite things to do are to go to the park and play sports like hockey, soccer, and basketball. I love to play with my dinosaurs, read dinosaur books and watch YouTube. Oh, and I love to draw with markers and stickers, too. My *mami* loves it when I draw her pictures.

I get to eat many different kinds of foods being two ethnicities. *Me encanta comer tacos de frijoles.* Dy, a little help for my friends, por favor. Dy says, "That means, I love to eat tacos made with beans." That is something that people in my *mami's* culture eat. You should try them sometime. They're really yummy.

Ice cream and paletas are so yummy too. "*Paletas* are fruity popsicles," Dy says.

My all-time favorite food to eat is fruit... all kinds of *fruta*! Remember, Dy told us earlier that *fruta* in Spanish means fruit.

I also love to eat many other foods like pizza, broccoli with rice, fried chicken and sweet potatoes. My g-mama makes yams sometimes, and I like those, too.

Today, *Mami* said we are going to visit my *abuelitos.* That means grandparents in Spanish, right Dy? We are also going to visit my g-parents. I love them all so much!

"Hurry and put your shoes on *papito*," my *mami* says. Dy, do you remember where I left my *zapatos*? *Zapatos* means *shoes* in Spanish. C'mon, let's start searching, Dy. We checked in our living room, and I didn't see them there. We scurried through the hallway and checked in our *cocina* and didn't see them there either. Oh yea, Dy says, "*cocina* means *kitchen*."

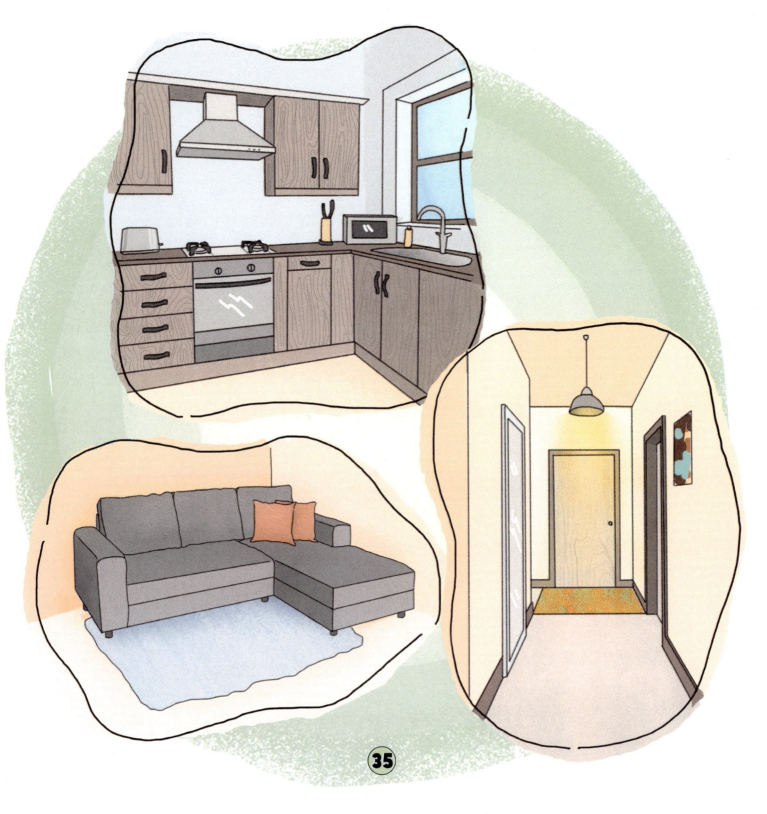

Hmm...where could they be? Dy and I hunt for the lost shoes. It's time for some serious detective work, Dy. We crept into my parents' room and found nothing. We climbed into the bathtub. "No shoes here," Dy says. Aha! I remember! I took them off in my room the last time I came home. C'mon Dy, let's go get them!

Found them! Oh, but here are my favorite kicks that my daddy bought me for my birthday. Which ones should I wear, Dy? My daddy and I have a lot of cool kicks. Sometimes I call them sneaks. Daddy says that gym shoes can also be called kicks. My Daddy teaches me new things all the time. Daddy is my hero! Heroes do great things when they teach other people new ideas. Me and daddy like to go shopping for new kicks from time to time and I love spending time with Daddy!

Ok Dy, I got my favorite red, blue, and white sneaks on. Let's go! I'm ready *mami*!

As I patiently wait for *mami* outside by the front door, I hear a loud thump coming from inside the house. Dy, what was that noise?

We ran to see what it was. As we turn the corner, my daddy comes hopping down the hall holding his foot. He is stammering some words out that sound like he's saying, "Ouch! Who left those building blocks on the floor?" Uh, oh! Dy, those are my lil' *hermanita's* building blocks. Oh, boy, is she in trouble! We have to go help her, Dy!

"NAOMI," Daddy yells. "Why did you leave your building blocks on the floor again?" Before my *hermanita* could say anything, I told daddy that I would help her pick them up so we can leave. Daddy smiled at me, gave me a pat on my head and said, "Ok little hero, go ahead and help your li'l sister."

Daddy called me a hero! Me??? Is that even possible? I guess it is. Maybe heroes do great things because they learned from all the OTHER heroes in their life.

Finally, we are *listos*! Ready to go! We ran to the car. I beat my hermanita, of course. And we were off to visit our *abuelitos* and g-parents.

ABOUT THE AUTHOR:

 Blanca Hines is a first time author who was born and raised in Illinois where her and her husband are also raising their two beautiful children. She is the founder of SHE Influences, a not-for-profit organization for women that helps create a support system for women to help them through their life journey.

Blanca's recent mission is to promote awareness for multi-cultural children and their parents on the importance of celebrating and exploring all cultures within a child's ethnicity. Through her books, she intends to sought out positive acceptance and understanding for children to not have to feel inferior over one race or another yet feel proud of the mixed culture they were born into.

Made in the USA
Columbia, SC
13 December 2020